# guys named Bill

Leslie Greentree

FRONTENAC HOUSE
Calgary

Lines quoted on p. 54 from "World Where You Live" and "Tombstone" by Neil Finn on the CD *Crowded House*, Capital Records 1986.

The publisher and author have made all customary and reasonable efforts to obtain permission from owners of previously copyrighted material. In the event that any copyright holder has inadvertently been missed the publisher will correct future editions.

Cover and Book Design by EPIX Design Inc.
Cover Illustration by Sam Weber.

Frontenac House acknowledges the support of Alberta Foundation for the Arts.

**National Library of Canada Cataloguing in Publication Data**

Greentree, Leslie.
  Guys named Bill


  (Quartet 2002)
  Poems.
  ISBN 0-9684903-6-0

  I. Title. II. Series.
  PS8563.R43G89 2002      C811'.6      C2002-910156-5
  PR9199.4.G73G89 2002

Printed and bound in Canada

Published by Frontenac House Ltd.
1138 Frontenac Avenue S.W.
Calgary, AB   T2T 1B6   Canada
Tel: (403) 245-2491  Fax: (403) 245-2380
E-mail: editor@frontenachouse.com
Website: www.frontenachouse.com

1 2 3 4 5 6 7 8 9   06 05 04 03 02

For SM

# acknowledgements

My heartfelt gratitude and affection to Blaine Newton and Kimmy Beach – both excellent writers and damn fun people – for their perceptive and intelligent criticisms, and for all the wine at Shauney's.

Thanks to Norm for understanding the difference between fact and fiction, and for supporting my writing.

Love and thanks to my family, for everything: Jerry, Rae Anne, Mike, Rian, Devony and Warren, Sheila and Russ, Tyler, Terry, Elise, Dominique, Sam, Shea and Mick.

Thank you to my friends and colleagues at Red Deer Public Library for their encouragement, especially to Debbie (aka Yaeger) and Leah for Australia.

Several of the poems in this book have been previously published – some in earlier versions – in *grain* and *Prairie Journal*. My gratitude to the editors.

Thanks to all the Bills.

# contents

**section III**

## guys named Bill

Rian and I step off the plane
breathing yellow hibiscus
tossing alohas to smiling swarthy men
they drape us with leis
kiss us on the cheek

I'm here to recover from Bill
shake myself clean at last
two weeks in which to re-enter the world
prepare myself for the man
who waits to buy me dinner
on our return

I did send Bill a postcard
from San Francisco airport –
something about a man in a dress
I don't know –
it was a layover    we were
sleep deprived and a little drunk

everyone in Hawaii is named Bill

we have our pictures taken
in Honolulu
glorious parrots astride each shoulder
the tousled man who chats us up
is Bill, the Parrot Guy

the bartender at our hotel
is Bill – Bill the Bartender
he loves us    it's nice to meet a
Bill who does
he puts extra rum in our Mai-tais
we laugh at his jokes

and then there's the night
we join a table of singing Australians
the dark-haired one with freckles
is Bill of the Australian Navy
I haven't kissed a man
in almost a year but
I'm used to kissing Bills

I've put away a lot of beer
with guys named Bill

# section I

## demons

our roommates were demons
waiting around corners
for our tiny feet to pad down the hall
in the night
to the toilet
they lived with us always
watching for weakness
alert to dreams they could enter stealthily
more real than God
because they showed themselves
occasionally

# caterpillar summers

you used to collect caterpillars
stroke their fuzzy bodies gently
laugh at the tickle as they inched up your skin
put them in a jar with careful air holes
feed them leaves, watch them eat
then came the summer of the caterpillars
everywhere, falling from trees
you couldn't play outside without
being covered in them
you would all stop playing to
pull them off each other
out of your hair, off your backs
for weeks you could hardly move
without squishing caterpillars against
your skin – bright yellow smears of guts
followed every wave of an arm
every scratch of the head left
sticky trails through your long brown hair
you stopped collecting them that summer
stopped feeding the ones you had
let them die in their jar

## the devil knows who I am

a black kitten
jumps onto my bed
I am drowsing
lying in the top bunk bed
we don't have a cat

I am seven
frightened calling for
my mother
it seems I have been
visited    I don't like
being selected
in this way

she asks if I want to
invite Jesus into
my heart
I nod through my
tears and we
whisper the magic words
the charm that will
hold the devil
at bay

at seven I don't
understand dreams
or talismans
but the devil
knows who I am

## Lamming Mills

it was your own Fern Hill
a magic hamlet tucked quietly in a corner of B.C.
no strangers, just dogs, children
crumbling old buildings
flowers sprouting everywhere
God just over the next hill
you were seven, then eight
bringing home fistfuls of forget-me-nots
daffodils and fireweed
buckets of tadpoles from the pond

you loved the neighbour boy
Bill was nine, with floppy blond bangs
falling on his freckled forehead
you loved him fiercely until he
asked you to marry him –
you hated him for two days until
he began to ignore you and it was safe
to yearn for him again

there were fairies, wild strawberries
there were moments you fit
seamlessly inside your child body
when being eight in Lamming Mills
was perfection and weightlessness
there was also the time you lost a bet
had to pull down your pants
show yourself to snickering boys
one day the rangers shot a bear out of a tree
in front of twenty sobbing children

you forget now that the mill was haunted
seeing endless summers
with vast night skies, shooting stars
wherever there is magic there are ghosts
old houses groan with voices and
this is where you first tasted
terror, longing, shame and joy
if God was around the corner
the Devil was there, in your room

you have never returned
afraid your adult eyes would see
only collapsing houses
the scum on the boiler pond
you try to remember freedom
and fear together
your childhood was peopled by
gods and ghosts
you still love men whose
hair flops over their foreheads

## torturer of worms

you were thirteen
you had a paper route
walking in the spring avoiding puddles
left by the rain
it was there in front of your careful feet
huge and green
worm or caterpillar –
doesn't matter – you have histories with both –
fat bright green with tentacle feet
it lies before you
raising the hair on your arms and
your stomach gives a little kick
your foot nudges it and the
huge green worm rolls into a puddle
thrashes around for what feels like forever
you watch it die slowly
you can't leave
you don't want to either –
you feel sick but glad
finally it sinks to the bottom of
the cloudy puddle
you can walk on
deliver those papers
avoid the chatty old man who stares at your breasts
but you keep seeing that thrashing green body
it comes to you at odd moments
puts the queasy feeling back in your stomach
you would do it again
you know it
you also know something else now
you may do everything else right
be a good girl
respect your elders and do your homework
but you are a torturer of worms

# God and your mom

He was waiting for you
you were told that
you didn't want God watching you patiently
waiting for you to tire of your shenanigans
you didn't want God and your mom to have
those little chats about you
even when they got to you and you
thought you were ready for surrender
you were steeling yourself against invasion
God and your mom saw your future:
peace, love, et cetera
you saw a Stepford wife
you would prefer to be pursued by demons
and you were, too
every misfortune a sign
every nightmare the devil's breath on your back
it was like a cheap horror flick
clear red horned evil behind you
as you crashed breathless through the woods
the eerie smile of benign hunger before you
no less terrifying
your mom the innocent dupe
crying *this way, this way*

## at the funeral

as children we saw the books
on witchcraft sitting on your shelf
in the small library with the sliding door
just off the living room
we would only enter in pairs –
the walls seemed to whisper otherwise
as adults we wondered at
the power of curses
imagining the uses hairs pulled from
our brushes were put to
or were the words enough?
as we sat at the funeral
tears rolling freely
we presented a picture of
a loving family
we said goodbye with
anger regret relief
wondering if this is what it takes
to break a curse

## at the wake

you often hear laughter at wakes
so we didn't stand out – my sisters and I
clustered in the group we have always formed
we had moved away from the trinkets
laid out for our choosing
holding our bits of costume jewelry
when one of us remarked
that all she wanted for a keepsake
was the wax doll formed in her image
so many years ago
and the pins to go with it
stifling our laughter
touching each other's arms protectively
we walked toward the wine
sobering only at the sight of our mother
clustered with her own sisters

## gestalt family

*you and those sisters of yours*
*you're a crazy bunch*
it was said in tones of admiration
we knew it    we shimmered
what was it about being together
they were all in love with us
we were in love with ourselves
I felt a sense of power
could feel myself growing larger
life becoming sharp-edged and brilliant
the uncles loved to dance with us
the aunts lavished hugs and laughter
cousins flirted    male and female
we were what they looked for at family events
I looked for myself at these events too
wondered where I was the rest of the year
when my sisters went home

## stranger

I didn't realize you were a stranger
until your brother died
two years of drinking and dancing
and I didn't know how
to say I'm sorry
I started watching you
saw how you held us at arms length
skillful    adept
no one else caught on but
I began to maneuver myself to your side
every woman loves a
good high fence
I made you love me through
sheer force of will

## the Devonian Gardens

I am thinking of a perfect day
the sky a pale autumn blue
breezes sweeping my hair across my face
so that you might gently brush it back
leaves crackled beneath our feet
strangers smiled at our happiness
I am thinking of the hardness of your thighs
pressed along the length of mine
your hands on my back as we stood
off the path, knee deep in wild grasses
we walked in flowers and butterflies
basked like lizards on sun-baked stones
I think of the bell in the Japanese Garden
we mounted the steps as though to an altar
preparing our wishes hand in hand
swinging together in silent ceremony
hearing the peal ring deep into
the heart of the day
I wished that I were the owner
not the beggarly borrower
of such joy

# 1987 –

*(for Bill)*

I craved you like a drink
spent years trying to crawl beneath your skin
swallow you from the inside out
those clouded hot days of
rum and lovely anger sat
embedded in my gut
a cancer I refused to fight
the feel of my fists
on your chest was the
solace that ushered me
finally, each night, into
dark dreamless sleep
I wished for your death some days
so I could fling myself
on your coffin screaming
find you always in the dirt
under my feet

# forms of salvation

alcohol didn't work; you went to church
same old story, priests must get tired of it
a love affair gone wrong, an
emptiness needing to be filled
the music was great – Rockin' with the Spirit
deep drums, bass mingled with the voices of angels
in too-tight polyester dresses
strangers wanting you, to hear your testimony
you held back, felt you were being
pried open with love
an older balding lonely man
shooting Jesus through his eyes
wanted you to let go
for your own good of course
said you look so cool
like butter wouldn't melt in your mouth
well how could you let go
with this King of Clichés
his hand moistly white on your arm
at least the drunks in the bar
don't pretend they're doing what they do to you
in the name of Christ

## first death

out of the dim bar into the night fuzzy with
rum and thick laughter a friend of a friend of
someone holding court on a low retaining wall
slightly familiar     leering with whiskey
breath and somehow in moments the
pleasantries shift and then there are
hands on you and you laugh pull away but they
tighten     try to wrench free without appearing
alarmed but something is happening
something is being proven and the hands
are large and strong     you are being twisted and your
fingers sink ineffectually into an oblivious
arm nails digging it is like a dream     you
are utterly without strength pulled held
in a steel embrace sky reeling     trying to
draw blood with cotton claws even as you
cling to your captor for balance without making a
sound among the smoking laughing hot dog
eating throng who ebb and flow blindly stumbling
to parked cars     you would hate to make
a scene after all it's like a joke a party
trick and you would hate to overreact now as you
flail helplessly silently within determined iron hands
sick with knowing finally released as the trophy
bra is waved and handed over     stuff
it in a pocket jam it down deep swaying trying
not to vomit     looking at the faces through
a haze marking somehow between ashen
gasps who is smiling and who is not  how you
get home is a mystery but the whole
night has become a mystery     there is a bed
to lie on eventually stare dry-eyed at the ceiling
for the eternity it takes a heart to
solidify in its new form     lay it out carefully
keep laying it out until the new shape takes

# my Pearl Harbor

I told Rian afterward that if this
Australian named Bill hadn't had that
wonderful vowelsome accent
if we hadn't met in a bar in Honolulu
if he hadn't invited us to a party
on an Australian naval vessel
hadn't brought me scotch then
bourbon with coke when I asked for rye
on the deck of a ship with waves lapping and
flowers scenting the air until
it felt like we were in a movie
if his name hadn't been Bill so that
it seemed fated somehow
I never would have looked at the guy twice
never would have kissed him under a bright moon
but all those strands converged
in Pearl Harbor that March when
my sister and I picked up a fleet of
Australian sailors in a bar
I know how that sounds but they were
singing Waltzing Matilda and
we had to join in    we knew all the words and
Canadian girls don't have that many
chances to use the word *billabong*
they were docked in Pearl Harbor
having run aground when
Nigel wasn't looking but
what better place to be dry-docked and
off they set to find two Canadian
girls looking for some laughs and some drinks and the
chance to see Pearl Harbor from a
different vantage point

I had never draped myself languorously
across anything before that night but
I draped myself over him like a breath
kissed him for hours
sweet and slow    recovering
regaining my footing in Pearl Harbor

## the only artist in the house

it's a heady feeling when you come together
the air crackles as you enter the room
a coven of dark haired laughing women
strangers stare and waiters dash over

it's hard to stand out surrounded by
creative, funny, vibrant sisters
sometimes you don't want to be part of something else
even when it's beautiful
sometimes you want to be the only one
like you in the room

we each have our roles
writer    artist    wife
but there is always someone encroaching
on the one or two things that make you special
you love being with them
but sometimes you can't breathe

when you meet a man with no imagination
you are drawn to him immediately
you will be the only artist in the house

# section II

## pastel symbolism

choosing a painting for the living room
is more difficult than choosing a husband
what it says about you is irrevocable
and what do you really want to say
after all   it can't just match the furniture
it needs to touch your heart
but there are two hearts in the house
and one wants a pretty golf scene
meanwhile you're musing about Greek gods
who resemble something that means something to you
you want pain and beauty and Yes –
this is Life, this is Art
and yet a tiny piece of you does want it to
match the furniture although entirely accidentally
you are frozen by your wish for pastel harmony and
your true desire for meaning in your
living room   the wall stays empty

# Bill Fish

after work we'd go across the street
to Bill's Fish Market
for a couple of drinks
it used to be a hair salon
rings still ground deep in the tile
from the old hydraulic chairs

Bill installed freezers for squid
prawns    Chilean sea bass
lobsters twitching through their tape
shelves of glistening bottles before mirrors
menus of cajun snapper
seafood stuffed eggplant and crawfish pie

we'd sit at the bar flirting with Bill
a jittery man fifteen years older
glad to see five young women come laughing
through the door he would sweep open
for us while he called the guy
behind us a dumb cunt

when the phone rang he would bark
*Bill Fish –*
*Christ Andy I'm up to my ass in orders*
*but sure I'll get that to ya*
he'd pour himself a scotch
winking as we told him about our day
he wasn't Bill Wyzykoski
Bill Fish – that was his name

some said he ran coke out of the back
but all I ever saw were coolers of
glistening salmon on ice
frosted glasses and cigar smoke
the regulars who straightened their collars
when we whirled in
relieved to float briefly somewhere
between our university classes and our
meaningless part-time jobs and our
itchy new roles as wives

Bill made my first martini
on the house
perfect and dry with two olives
watched me drink it like a
parent taking off the training wheels
one day he said to me
*you're a classy dame*
it hardly took away from it when he
leaned over and licked my face

# euchre Sundays

when I was talking about this poem
and the euchre tournaments that inspired it
someone suggested I change it to canasta   saying
*euchre's not poetic*
*canasta   now that's a poetic sounding card game*
but it was euchre we played
the last Sunday of every month
at Bill's Fish Market

the great thing about Bill's was I could
go there when I was alone
pretend I was looking for halibut
allow myself to be pulled in
Bill Fish would draw me a red-eye
tell dirty jokes while I settled in
for the afternoon and bummed a smoke

it's a game the players are proud of knowing
the day I walked in to Bill's and asked what
they were playing they told me gently
*you won't know it   it's an eastern game*
when I said
*looks like euchre*
there was great rejoicing and the beer
keg opened before me and the men in
the room shouted for joy
I pulled up a chair and won their money
and thus the great monthly
euchre tournament was born

Rob was unemployed for two years
he quit Wal-Mart because he couldn't stand
that fucking cheer every morning
oh, he made some beautiful lone hands

Wally was the survivor of two triple bypasses
and a heart transplant
swilling scotch and smoking cigars
calling trump if he had one in his hand

Bill Fish was the hero
galloping in with the audacious call
every hand a hill to die on
he'd get up to sell prawns or oysters
come back to find we'd killed him
and needed more beer

I was *Our Fourth*
that's what they shouted every time I
walked through the door
I spent my winnings
every euchre Sunday
on beer and cheese sticks

# death of a good man

it was an odd movie
the heroine cool, aloof, difficult to pin down
her husband was attentive, appeared loving
she planned his murder with
elegance
we watched silently, rapt
as the credits rolled, my husband
turned to me in confusion and frustration
*why, why would she want him to die*
*she didn't have a lover*
*he did everything right*
*he loved her   I don't understand ...*
I shrugged in apparent perplexity
holding my smile inside
wasn't it reason enough simply
that he was her husband?

# Whyte Avenue

we walk hand in hand, I'm almost bouncing beside you
like a teenager skipping school
laughter spills from the patio tables
ahead of us a man in a straw hat tosses money
at the feet of a mime who
comes to life at the clink of coins
whirring   buzzing   machine-like
the man in the straw hat strides on
looking back over his shoulder
laughing in delight
the look on his face makes me laugh too
and I love this stranger in the straw hat
we are momentarily united in the
goodness of the day
I hug your arm across my breast

we enter the cool of a used bookstore
wander the aisles stroking the spines
follow a winding staircase to magazines
cracked titles under glass
I see the man in the straw hat
wonder if I'm brave enough to say hello
but it's that sort of day
if we were in a bar I would send him a beer
I see the magazine he holds –
red gash of flesh like a wound
cocks fingers tongues splayed
caricature of a woman in the hands of
the man in the straw hat
when you reach for me I brush past your hands
pretend not to see

# lessons of lying

I have become a liar
not a good one, but
the evasions and omissions
I employ to avoid detection
pass unnoticed
I fumble along my tightrope
playing to an audience that
is no longer there, or is
looking elsewhere for clowns or popcorn
becoming a liar has demonstrated
my irrelevance
my invisibility
while they began as simple lies
they have become assertions
breeding the need for more

# behind the seventeenth green

some young guy at a golf tournament
laughs at a couple of your jokes
and suddenly the air changes
you realize he is watching you and
the beer is crisp on your tongue
the sun warm on your back
when you think back on this day later
you try to clutch at how you felt
you forgot you were a wife
became the person you saw in his eyes
when he kissed you
behind the seventeenth green
you waited a long moment
before pulling away
really, you tell yourself
what was the harm
you had a little fun
felt sick to your stomach with
longing for six weeks

## when cobras mate

Sunday evening, bored out of my mind with
my house, him, with the ceaseless parade of
drab meals I throw together
flipping through channels impatiently
waiting for my life to begin again Monday morning
outside this barren place
a nature show caught me
two King Cobras, mating
my breath stopped at their languid grace and
I wanted to twine myself around you
in just that sinuous way
curving and sliding together
showing you my throat
the camera closed in
on the crimson penis:
a spent flower slowly furling
I said  *look, how beautiful*
but I was sitting in the wrong room
with the wrong person and it became
one more wasted moment

## fairy tale

you have worn me down
like a rock in a river, slowly
until one day
I have no edges left
a smooth, miscellaneous stone
submerged in the same grey trickle that has
eroded countless others into inertia
you have taken me
as if you were a king
and I a peasant virgin
it looks like a fairy tale
if one doesn't stop to think that
those without
never catch up to
those who hold it all
those who walk indifferently by rivers
throwing stones casually into currents
while thinking of other things

## shopping on a Wednesday

it happens when you stop waiting for it
when you no longer have the words prepared
or your hair done just right
it happens when you are leaning over the bread
in the aisle of the grocery store
hair hanging over your face
thinking of pork chops and rice
and there he is, smiling with the full
blueness of those eyes
as you stand slightly bent, eyes wide, mouth open
no longer capable of picking up a conversation
set aside regretfully a year earlier
so you babble stupidly and leave unsaid
all the words you practised
leave him to wonder why he ever thought you were
funny, special, interesting, beautiful
so you go home and separate your meat
and put things away in the wrong places
and wander around your house for hours
thinking of all the things you have stopped waiting for

## march of worms

small grey worms crawl up the south-facing wall
rough dull grey with suction-cup heads
plodding all those worm-miles to the roof
I flick them off with a fingernail
the next morning there are more
and again the next
halfway up the house
I begin to kill them –
squashing small grey smears
against the white siding
I run the barbeque lighter
under three of them
watch their tiny bodies
stiffen and shrivel instantly
disconnect from the siding and fall to the ground
but there are more every morning
propelled mindlessly to the eaves
I search the library for worms
garden pests, pest control, larvae
shudder over countless photographs
but none of my particular worms
I spray the siding with Raid –
they drop like pellets
only to be replaced within the hour
I don't know what to do
I check the wall continually
lie in bed staring at the ceiling above me
wondering if above my pretty peach walls
with the crisp white trim
there lies an attic writhing with nameless grey worms

## things found hidden at the back of bookshelves

so this is what you desire –
to push me roughly to the floor
holding yourself triumphantly
like a club
do you wish I had
blood red fingernails to scratch you and do you
call me babe
or bitch
imagine holding my head
hard against your thighs
would you pretend not to notice me gag
or would your vacant eyes see nothing but
the movie rolling in your mind
would you remember my name
my position in your life
or are you looking for trophies
glistening streams running down my face
scarlet lipstick rings
at the base of your cock

## flesh and bone

standing naked at the mirror
I examine my pale cool skin
the way it lies transparent over bone

the grooves in my forehead
are no longer smoothed away
by your touch

we have both abandoned my body

I trace the blue lines on my wrist
press it to the cold glass
I have all the time in the world to decide
which is the greater loneliness

## my straight man

I thought it would be funny to tell you
I was in love with another man
you would know from my smile
there was a punch-line
I would tell you he's a literary character
he doesn't really exist
you would say
*oh well then I guess I have nothing to worry about*

you barely glance up from the paper
I am driven to these cheap tactics
trying to make you look at me
but you refuse to be my straight man
next time I might have to bring in the neighbour
have sex with her on the kitchen floor
right in front of you
I grow more outrageous
a small child tugging at your pantleg

# almost twenty-one again

we're still friends
to prove it every two years or so
I breeze into town
take them all out for a game of golf
beer and laughter
pulling each other
back in time until
we are almost twenty-one again

I've learned some things in the
last twelve years
I can out-drive them now
fart jokes are no longer funny
although I smile and quaff my beer
eager to be sucked back into
the swirl of smoke and booze

this is all a prelude to the
post-game cocktails
the eventual movement to a bar where
after dancing with the others
I will place myself in Bill's arms
close my eyes and sink into his
hard chest until he kisses me

# love letters

you knew he hated loving you
would forget you in a second if he could
spent four years trying to
dismiss your persistent dogged faith
you see how that led you grateful
to someone who could say the words out loud
but you knew it wasn't over
you would always be the force to be resisted
biding your time until one dark beer-drenched night
realigns the heavens
and you claim your right
thirsty kisses pulled from you
strewn back at your feet like gifts in a truck by a lake
for two weeks you are drunk    giddy
whispers in the night    secrets
skin crawling with hunger
with triumph
you understand
when you catch yourself editing his love letters

## after you left

you should have washed your hands
before you left me
how will you explain the scent of
my naked need
on your fingers
or the wine on your breath
I washed nothing     went outside
placed a cigarette carefully in my lips
lit it     drew it deep into me
looking at the evergreens
seeing for the first time the pale
new fringe of mint green growth
edging the dull dark needles

## marked

a bruise the size of a plum
graces my left hip
the one mark I took
from our encounter

the blooming purple
is fading now to a matte brown

tracing the outline with a solitary finger
I wonder if you went home and
climbed on your wife to relieve the pressure
I lit the barbeque
carefully placing a steak above
the glowing coals
licking the raw red juice from my fingers

# what I should have said

in your arms, in your truck
your words and your hands running over me
like poetry    through me
filling and opening me
as I sink warm and inarticulate
into the amber of your eyes
unable to say that you are the undercurrent
tugging me as I move through my day
that when I am alone
my fingers move to the places
you have touched me
my throat    my heart
that something inside me rises
like a red balloon
or a white flag
when I see you
a recognition    an answer to
questions I have not asked
this is what I should have said
it didn't seem beautiful enough for you

## Neil Finn sings

I'm running in place
on the treadmill you bought me for
stress relief and slenderness
isn't that what wives do
Neil Finn sings in my headphones
*we're looking for wide open spaces*
*high above the kitchen*
you are upstairs on the computer
I sweat subversively
in the basement
*we are neither at home nor at work*
Neil and I
*we are moving*
Neil is giving me oceans and thunder
the hills are breathing
we are building my running legs
building my anthems
painting me a flag

## taking a message

I think I just spoke to your next wife
she called with a business question
only you could answer
I was polite
didn't say what bad form she showed
not waiting for the body to cool
but then maybe she knows the body
has been like ice for years
I was polite
managed to keep warmth from my voice
some habits are hard to break
I used to think she liked me
before realizing she was waiting
for my husband
circling our dying marriage like a
hungry young magpie
I told her to take care

## a new bed

never having subscribed to revenge shopping or shopping to
fill a void in one's life or shopping to distract one from how
thoroughly unloved one might be still today I walked into a
store decisive angry and bought a bed     I was not there long
I spent approximately one hundred dollars a minute pulled
out my shiny new credit card signed my shiny new name
stroked the plastic covered mattress with hatred and
satisfaction     vowed to my unstained new bed that it would
never shake with raucous snores or be the site of fucking
passing as love in the eyes of a girl so dazzled by a tasteful
tie collection she never thought to ask who chose them     I
chose a headboard that doesn't match the furniture I have
been allotted     murmuring to myself that within the year
the rest will be kindling and my new bed and I will start
again     it will settle softly under my solitary breathing
perhaps lead me into peaceful sleep

# Section III

## assembly of a bed

you offered to help me assemble my new bed
that was kind of you
I almost let you but I thought I might as well
learn right now
how to do everything myself
learn how to be alone and not pathetic about it
that's a heavy load of equipment to haul around a house
I skinned my knuckles
bloodied a couple of them
taught the dog a few new curses
cracked a beer     went back at it
the first screw is always the scariest
the frame was crooked     I pulled things apart
tried again
got it straight
opened another beer
checked widths et cetera with the tape measure I
bought yesterday
wrenched those bolts as tight as I could
swung that bitch of a box spring around without taking
out the ceiling fan
pulled the mattress into place
those chunks of metal became a bed
and mine were the only hands to touch it
I made it up with care
smoothed the freshly laundered linens like a benediction
lay across it with my beer

# the prettiest one in the room

I look good –
slim black dress
hair pulled into an
elegant twist
one more wedding
drinking wine as fast as I can
my social smile in place
the best man is smiling at me
happy to be speaking to
a pretty girl
although we both know he's the
prettiest one in the room
I let him tell me I look fantastic
his wife just gave birth and is
still lumpy
sitting in the corner with her
nursing pads and her red
wrinkled baby and a cluster
of admiring women
I prefer to drink wine
toss my hair at her husband
I look at her soft stomach
the blue bruises under her eyes
motherhood is beating the
crap out of her already and her
husband wants to fuck me

## hanging pictures

I'm hanging pictures in my new place
the same ones we once hung together
you were visiting for the weekend
my husband not home yet
he always took his time
even when one of his oldest friends was visiting
we barely noticed
I triumphant with my purchases of the day
designed to make this new house a home
you laughing   hammer and nails in hand
we spent an hour deciding where they should hang
you full of ideas and advice
that I ultimately ignored
but I loved the way you pitched in
held them against the wall
moved them infinitesimally   obediently
like a brother
when he arrived home we displayed our work proudly
beers in hand    conspirators
now in my new home
a place you have not seen and never will
I'm hanging my pictures alone
balanced precariously on the bed
nails in my teeth
when I think of you and
understand finally that you too are gone

## John the Baptist

he's preaching on the street corner again
beside the stone statue of
Clydesdales pulling a fire wagon
I don't know what he's saying
but I see the passion in his
wild gesticulating arms
Elvis hair with Johnny Cash clothes
an hour later he's in the library
his buddy walks over says
*hey man I saw you out there*
waves casually toward the street
John the Baptist smirks at him
says *yeah*
he rolls his eyes like it's his job
he's not really that crazy about it
but what's a guy to do

# Saturday night

the aluminum plant is shedding again    it's Saturday night
you've poured your third vodka as you deadhead all the
plants in the place you need more plants    it's only nine
o'clock and time can weigh a little heavy when you're
walking around the house in your underwear drinking vodka
certain no one would look through your open window at the
rows of luscious repotted plants    not a brown leaf in sight
or at your bare breasts as you pace the floor sipping your
drink hoping for a storm    something to break the silence
the monotony    at least the thunder shakes every house you
won't be alone    in a storm everyone is alone    pour
yourself another drink and think of amusing stories to tell at
work on Monday for God's sake don't talk about the plants

# Jesus in the library

I met him at work
the telephone was ringing
books in hand, I hurried
through the library

he sprang toward me
a faint sour smell
electric curls falling around
his shoulders, eyes
beaming with love

he was supposed to talk to me

it took me a moment to
realize Jesus had instructed him
to seek me out
I turned, furious
almost running from
his shining eyes

don't think you're the
first one Jesus has
pointed me out to, buddy

why does he never send
you people to the old woman with
the hump who farts audibly
among the stacks?

two years later I wonder
when he doesn't show up
for a few weeks

I bet Jesus looked just as
crazy to non-believers

# righteous acts like filthy rags

I stand in the grip of
serious pain     sweating with it
wondering what the
hell I'm doing here when
every ounce of blood I possess is
being expelled so viciously
the congregation sings
lustily and I grab the chair
in front of me

once a month for two days
I think I'm going to
die and apparently attending
church doesn't help and for
shit's sake it's the third time in as
many months the sermon is
dedicated to tithing more
than you earn and trusting that
you will be cared for
and frankly the constant mention of
blood is making me nauseous
though I acknowledge the
context is quite different

oh Lord that huge lonely loud woman
with the browning teeth just
caught my eye she's staring and
her face lights up with purpose
I look straight ahead try to
wipe the grimace of agony
from my face but she's
shouldering through the crowd
I can vaguely hear her through the
haze of pain and electric guitars

God has spoken to her    I need prayer

*all I really need is an Advil*
I say    pulling away from the
unwashed smell and the unbrushed
teeth so close to my face
she is drawing me into her
Christian embrace    I'm holding my
breath she's praying for
me and I'm praying just as hard

*oh Lord please don't let me vomit in church in front of everyone*
*Lord please get this creature off me  please oh please before I throw*
*up everywhere get her off me God oh please*

I finally have the
wit to thank her and    .
now her job is done
she can go home this
afternoon grateful for her gifts
compassion mercy healing fingers
for hearing the voice of God
I can go home peel the
bloodied cotton from my
sticky thighs throw it
in the garbage curl up and
sleep for three hours

# blasphemer

the women at work shake their heads
*after twenty years*
*out of the blue*
*he comes home and tells her he's leaving*
*she can't believe it*

Laura's husband left her when the son
he wanted so badly was two months old
*they're all filthy bastards*

Bev says
*you hear about this kind of thing all the time*
*one day they just up and leave*
*it makes you want to lock them in the*
*house after they turn forty*

I am the blasphemer
*nothing is out of the blue*
*nothing*
twenty years of silence
or twenty years of bickering
that barely concealed rolling of the eyes
when hearing the same stupid stories
at every party
withholding sex and/or money amid
perfunctory pecks on the cheek
*I love you* ticked off the daily chore list
first thing, so you don't forget

she's a liar
*nothing is out of the blue*
*if you're paying attention*
*and if you're not*
*well then*

the women are shaking their heads
I'm thinking
*run, buddy, run*

# dinner parties

I'm trying not to imagine you pouring wine
for your guests     laughing
you probably bend over to kiss her briefly
you know that's what women want

I know I wanted it     I waited for it
created meals like an artist
baring my weakness in leg of lamb
with orzo and Greek salad
paella curry angelhair pasta

as I placed the plates
before them with that smooth
self-effacing flourish all women know
the need for my guests to believe I was
loved was all that mattered

I'm sure you offer the gift
of a brief touch on her shoulder
as you clear the dishes
you are interesting and amusing
wishing you were somewhere else
but committed to the appearance of normalcy

I'm counting up losses and
glasses of wine on a Saturday night
aligning my asparagus tips on the plate
toying with my salmon

## postcard from Mexico

I can see you walking
the curve of beach below the hotel
ankle deep in surf

I don't miss Mexico
we slept in separate beds for a week
I waited for you to come to me
we pretended it was a joke

you went to bed early most nights
I sat on the deck with an Australian
smoking and drinking
watching the stars and shooting the shit

he walked me to our room at three a.m.
it was strange to be seen that way
as a woman who should be walked home
a woman requiring care

one moment stands out for me
when I think of Mexico
I was sick on the golf course and
you were kind    I was surprised by that
and grateful enough to continue playing
instead of asking to be taken back to the room

it amazes me now
that you never saw the pattern
never understood that a kind word or two
was enough to make me shrug off pain
I would have crawled that golf course
to have you look at me so gently

## mid-winter holiday

thanks for the postcard
Mexico looks lovely as usual
this year for my mid-winter holiday
I chose a monastery in Saskatchewan
where chickadees alight on my naked palm
there are no palm trees here
just a library with books older than Canada
no sandy beaches either
just a snowy forest with a large pink
shrine to the Virgin Mary
about the time you're teeing off on the eighth hole
I'm meeting Kimmy for pre-lunch cocktails
and when you're lounging by the pool
watching the bikinis saunter by
we are in the midst of our
mid-afternoon shooter break
reading our new poems aloud
as you soak in the Jacuzzi
we are stretched across monastic cots
sipping wine before vespers
easing our computer cricks
I'm sure you turn up your nose at the local cuisine
last night I ate liver
for the first time in twenty-two years
played three games of pool with a monk
I wake each morning to the bells for Lauds
sleep each night in a narrow bed
in an austere room
I will not return to Mexico
I holiday with poets now
I sample the wines of the world alphabetically

# talking to the dog at midnight

it descends on you
this writer's frenzy
one compliment and you're sitting up
till all hours when you have to
work in the morning
scribbling crazily
drunk on praise
it made you feel like a writer
made you even say the words aloud
out there in your yard
with your foolscap and your pencil with the
clicking extendable lead you said
*I am a writer* and laughed at your dog
as he wandered the yard
keeping an eye on you
it made you want to grab the closest stranger
kiss him hard
you pour yourself a vodka but
hardly touch it for the words spilling
out of your fingers
you are a thief
robbing your memories
hoping you don't wake in the morning and
see this for the crazy drunken euphoria
it feels like
you don't want to go to sleep
for that very reason you want to sit up forever

# back to Australia

*(via 67th Street)*

we spent months in Australia
we're supposed to be working our way
around the world, alphabetically
we've moved on through Brazil, Chile
but I'm walking along telling
Leah how much I wish
we were back in Australia
when Yaeger comes up behind us and
whispers *I miss Australia*
that's all it takes and back we walk
through the 67th Street Liquor Store
to those hearty reds
and we're gone     we're not the world
travelers we tried to be but there's
something about Australia that
fits with the old trunk in my house
covered with candles and ivy
the pewter wine rack and the carafes
we bought each other     something that fits
with the Vietnamese food we order in and
the ex-husband stories we like to tell as
we drink with handmade wineglasses
from Muenster, Saskatchewan
we are back, in Australia

## our sommelier

he paces frantically removes his glasses to
replace them seconds later
as he explains the nuances of
merlots and cabernets
we breathe    we sip    we swish

it's a different theme each month
fabulous reds    France    Spain
ports and brandies in December
next month we're doing Australia
we talked him into it
with ease    with a smile
a laughing shake of the hair as we
dropped phrases like
legs    body    berries

last month we traveled two hours
to a wine-tasting
also starring our sommelier
dressed ourselves in black
placed silver at our necks
pretended not to notice men
circling as we licked
paté from our fingers

a man in a hand-painted tie wanted to
buy me dinner
I told him I was still bitter    not ready
I was also taller than him
and I escaped to the side of our sommelier
he put his arm around me for a moment
I leaned in to his warm bulk

if you pretend something long
enough you become it
I am taller now

our sommelier's name is William
but I like to call him Bill

## your name

I think of you
above me
your hand heavy
on my forehead
pushing back my
tangled hair
your dark eyes
on my face
on my mouth as
it forms
your name

## charcoal drawing

I want to draw you with a charcoal pencil
lying on your side, the merest suggestion of
crumpled sheets beneath you
I will create the line from your chest to your thigh in
one flowing movement
smudging into the hollow of your hipbone a
shadow the size of the heel of my hand
shading softly the ribs jutting through your
pale skin, the valley below your rib cage
tracing carefully the brown of your nipples
your arms will be outstretched
hands open, fingers slightly curved
I will use an entire pencil on your eyes
darkening, then darkening them again
stroking clean lines on your jaw
feathering grey shadows along the bones of your face
running my thumb over the cheekbones
to soften the lines
I will name each part aloud
as I draw it, rolling the words around in my mouth
running my tongue over each sound

Leslie Greentree lives in Red Deer, Alberta, and works as an Information Services Assistant at Red Deer Public Library, which means that, when she's not writing, she is looking up obscure and interesting facts. When she's not doing either, she attends a lot of wine tastings.